Funny Poems for Everyone!

by Marcus Ten Low

Volume 4

Funny Poems for Everyone! – Vol. 4

© 2025 Marcus Ten Low

All rights reserved.

No part of this publication may be reproduced, stored in a retrieval system, or transmitted in any form or by any means, electronic, mechanical, photocopying, recording, or otherwise, without the prior written permission of the copyright holder, except for brief quotations embodied in critical articles or reviews.

First published in Australia by Marcus Ten Low

ISBN: 978-0-9577768-5-2

Cover and interior design by Marcus Ten Low

The included poem 'I did not see the cat' first appeared on the *Australian Children's Poetry* website.

For rights, permissions, or other enquiries, contact: marcustenlow@gmail.com

Welcome!

A warm hello to all my readers, or anyone who has chanced upon this very lucky, very imaginative book.

Here are a fourth set of funny poems, but these are more surprising, mostly longer, and even more beautifully color-illustrated poems, that will delight you even more than the last!

I created the bulk of these poems with illustrations in a few intensive weeks in winter of 2025, at home and in some of the public libraries of the city of Meanjin/Brisbane, Australia, where I have been based since mid-2015.

May my poems ever free your imaginative spirits! Happy reading!

Contents

Big Susie's visit	6
Treasured handkerchief	9
Our lemonade stand	11
Rat in the poker machines	12
The tipsy man	14
Babies, babies	17
My caped superhero	18
The famous soup	21
The court hearing	22
My grandfather	24
Quiz show	26
The tightrope walker	27
The gargoyle	29
Beach ball play	31
Widdershins	33
I did not see the cat	34
Between the shelves	37
Her worms and her squirms	38
Pig over the oceans	40
Me, the old man, and the kite	43
The adept percussionist	44
The mad man at christmas	45
The televised lovers	46
Who stole my hat?	48
The street broker	51
The zebra in the city	52
A realist's valentine poem	54
Rapacious pizza	55
The poisoned fish	56

The man from Timbuktu	57
Rules of the snack machine	59
Appraising the statues	60
The lost mathematical proof	62
The terrarium experiment	64
The forlorn seamstress	66
Rising of the phoenix	67
Man changes lightbulb	69
Most ridiculous recipe	70
The wandering piper	73
The old man's will	74
About the creator	77

Big Susie's visit

As I make scones with jam to fit,
Big Susie eat them in a trice!
She licks her lips and primps a bit,
And says plumply, "They're very nice."

She cleans the cream left on her arm,
Then opens up the window view:
My flower garden's quite a charm,
My roses red, and violets blue.

She goes outside and pads around,
Looking into the neighbor's yard;
They have a pool where one boy drowned,
Which Susie makes her way toward.

With wicked legs and arms she mounts
Precariously the rotting fence;
The fence breaks off in small amounts,
Or bends with little in defence;

And Susie lands feet first and limbs
Upon the home of Messrs Noyes.
She strips half-naked, and then swims
The pool's length, with its blow-up toys.

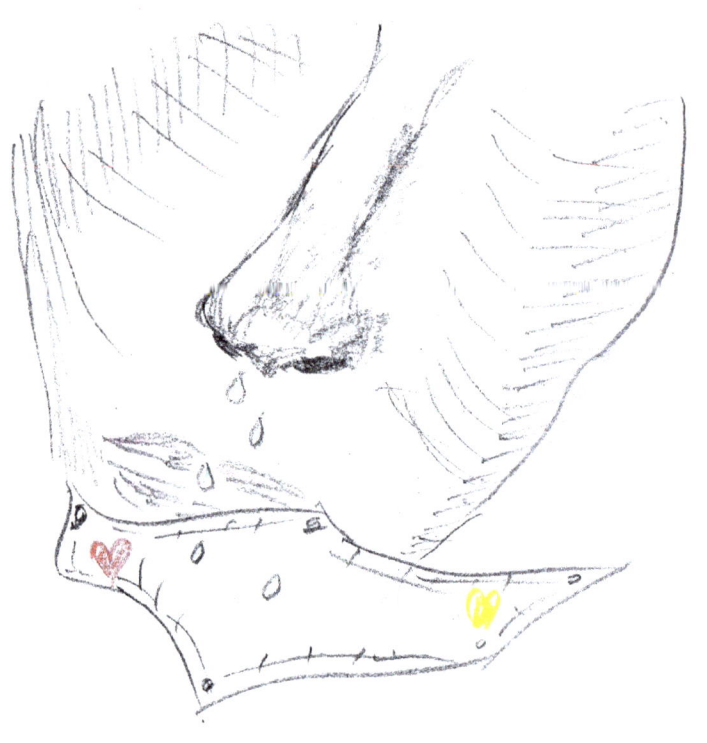

Treasured handkerchief

On Desdemona's handkerchief, I drew
The wild map to a grim man's brooding heart:
Containing neither tears wept like the dew,
Nor dancing like some vapid, abstract art;

Instead, the surging rivers of desire,
The beauty of a silent mask unstuck,
Met with the fiercest instruments of fire,
The coursing passions, or love's pure gold struck.

The kerchief fluttered, flagging, such a charm
Yet too, too simply blown apart by grief:
The blowing of the nose, fuzzy and warm,
The falling of its folds like autumn leaf.

Th' opening of this piece is ne'er the same,
The fluid in it's dried, it's old and torn:
Now that the thing is dirty, caked, and lame,
It should be then discarded and forsworn.

Our lemonade stand

I had a Great American Dream, and woke up with a fright.
For one thing, I had peed in bed, staining it overnight.

Outside my window, lemons on the lemon tree looked nice,
And so I went and carried in a few, to chop and slice.

I boiled sugar and water, and I squeezed the lemons in,
Then found some things, a sign, a stand, and a collection tin;

"5 cents for lemonade," I wrote, with all the cups set out;
Fran taste-tested the lemonade, and gave a little pout,

Then got hiccups, but found a way to let her sorrows drown;
And then the chilly breeze came out, and knocked all our cups down,

And neighbors came and asked whether we had our own insurance,
And others claimed, beside our mess, that we kids lacked endurance;

And just as we began to pack up with our heavy hearts,
An entourage of travellers cruised past, not from these parts,

And they were hella thirsty, and the lemonade they loved—
They gave us fifty dollars, so our sales had just improved.

With all this cash, we gloated and opted to raise the price;
And though the lemons had run out, we just put in more ice,

And made each cup a little smaller, but still looking fine,
A bit like Coca-Cola, and their mass production line.

So next time you are giving up, and going back to bed,
When life gives you some lemons, make some lemonade instead.

Rat in the poker machines

Ooh look! here's a squirming, a scrabbling rat!
Running around inside these coin-slot machines,
The poker machines that I stay seated at!
All-grinning like this is an ad for Macleans!

As I spin the wheel with one firm tug of the lever,
Mister Rat runs the rounds and the whirligig thing!
The wheel seems to spin on for ever and ever,
But as it slows down, I can see the rat cling

To any gear, joint, or cog in the machine—
And a few other gamblers pass me and my rat,
But none see him wave at me from 'neath the screen!
And then—of a sudden, a rat-a-tat-tat!!

(That's the sound of a payout into my coin tray.)
Three cherries aligned means I score a nice win—
I'm suddenly rich thanks to this rat's bold play!—
Then the rat disappears, in the midst of this din!!

As I bundle my prize, with the staring of eyes
All around me, I give thanks to this splendid rat,
The hero of this tale despite his small size;
Hoping he should come back, and I'll give him a pat!

The tipsy man

He wrapped his fat arms around me,
So giddy with such glee, such glee,
Spilling a good half of his beer
Upon those walking fairly near;

He dialled the number to get more,
Plus pizza and some lava cake,
And roused himself to dance the floor,
Shaking around like some earthquake—

He leapt upon a wooden chair,
And did the karaoke there;
I must admit, his voice was great,
If that's something I must relate—

When suddenly he slipped and fell,
Injured himself—and fraught with moans,
He gripped my legs, till I as well
Was floored, against his broken bones.

Babies, babies

Crawling along up every wall,
In through the doors and crevices,
A few who bawl and bawl and bawl,
Invaders of the premises!

O, babies, babies, everywhere!
As I turn every corner, more
At every rail, on every stair!
Oozing along each corridor!

Sitting so plump in front of screens
That flicker with the morning news,
The babies babble, made with genes
Of parents in their different hues,

Leaking their messes on the floor!
Clutching at airs, some much too bold
That one day, they'll wage vicious war
Over the Earth, and turn so old...

My caped superhero

While others plainly do adore,
My boy's no caped hero at all;
But I myself am not so sure—
His face smashes into the wall

And turns out looking pretty pert;
Pieces of wall flutter his eyes,
Whilst his comments are pretty curt;
Away, away he vainly flies;

He drives a chair pulled on its side,
He chucks pronged objects through the air
Which stick on passers in their stride;
He falls off, rolls, stands with a glare.

Yet by man's deeds a man's recoup
Is judged in such a proud display;
He wraps himself in one fell swoop,
And trundles off, and off, away.

The famous soup

Two teens, with soup cans hidden in their coats,
Stood by the *Mona Lisa*—in that vast place,
The Louvre—pretending to idle—sprung like stoats,
They leapt upon 't, and on her smiling face

Threw all the soup upon her, to the gasps
Of bystanders around, all gripped with fear!
The two yelled, "Just Stop Oil!" in angry rasps,
Now rooted to the spot, with filming near;

O, while the two rascals were soon arrested,
The footage of this scene was smuggled out,
And aired on social media, attested
By th' many—and the brand of soup they'd bought

Were thrilled to give them more, even in jail,
Where they both dwelled for months, held for their crime!
And that same soup at once appeared for sale
Everywhere, loved by camp kids in winter clime

And many a family household, just as well,
Until, at last, the proud soup company
Started to feed the homeless, those who dwell
By shopfront, bridge, or park—without a fee!

So next time you open that can of soup,
Loving its taste, with more soup on the boil—
Know that it started with a teenage coup,
To rid the world of th' corruption caused by oil.

The court hearing

Charged with some crimes, I wandered into court
One dismal day, my mind consumed with thought
Like, "What will I have today for my lunch?"
I thought I had a certain, certain hunch—

Yeah nah, I had in fact been pulled in here
Through tunnels from the police watchhouse near,
Where echoes of the many accused's voices
Moan with the rank denial of their choices.

And as the lawyer whom I'd been assigned
Bowed low before the high-placed magistrate,
We'd not discussed at all my "specious" mind
(*Mens rea*, as they love to demonstrate)—

And so distracted, I looked round the room,
And th' flowers outside, dancing in pretty bloom;
The judge's voice was half a mile away,
As more of th' audience gathered at the fray.

A baby, held among them, started crying,
When its stuck mother dropped one of her earrings
Onto the floor; but inside, I was dying
To get to th' very end of all my hearings—

And to this end, I shouted from my lungs,
"Your Honor, I simply cannot HEAR you!!"
The judge spoke hoarsely and, in bitter tongues,
Ordered that I, with baby now in view,

Be taken from this most despondent scene:
And, lo and behold, the baby did a poo
While breastfeeding, or something in between;
But, anyway, the rest was gobbledegoo...

Ya know, most people are like pretty flowers:
In need of love, and song, and sometime showers;
And if, from time to time, they do things wrong,
Please...give them something GOOD to live among.

My grandfather

My grandfather, like some old clock
Carved out of one old, mighty oak,

Who sat there: strange, old man with cloak
Under another, God-wrought tree;

That when he yelled, with each tick-tock,
That while he ached, his grave wealth spoke

With each cold foot wrapped in each sock
Beneath the folds of gallantry;

His tongue, his chosen tie like pendulum,
His naked breath upon my face's scum,

His arms around my neck, his eyebrows woke
And grey, his voice so thick, so slick, so broke;

Or when he mentioned virtue, like some rot
His many oafish sons, they all forgot—

Struck once by lightning, on his piebald head!
He fell, and was immediately dead—

Averting blame, I scurried off in haste,
As eager birds came pecking at his waste.

Quiz show

Quiz show! Quiz show! The compere is well-paid,
And, please know, has more chance of getting laid—
And while he riles contestants with a smile,
Once losers leave, he sends them off in style.

The more they win at first, the more's the chance
They'll risk it all at some point, to advance:
With such great risk, great opportunity—
But nothing is for free, quite seriously.

Oh, that the host struts in his smart blue suit,
With prizes like a car, a cruise, or loot—
The real prize is the moment of your fame,
And all the thrill to be part of the game.

The tightrope walker

Young Johnny Balance, champion of the world!
One day he tried to walk a tightrope strung
Between two tallest towers—feet unfurled
Upon its length; to his long pole he clung,

Venturing out, at last tasting the breeze...
Halfway across, his twitchy nose felt raw—
He let go of the pole, with one huge SNEEZE!!
The pole fell a long way, and pierced the floor

Below, of some old garage of spare parts,
While Johnny clung to th' tightrope high above.
And oh, he clung and clung, e'en as the charts
Of stars emerged, and (with nothing to prove)

Some birds appeared, and landed on his head!
They pooped on him, then thought again to fly,
As someone on the ground looked up in dread!
Someone had spotted him, caught in the sky!

No helicopters were flying in sight,
So she called for a fire truck nearby—
Whose fighters took their time but, in their plight,
Brought out a trampoline so capably!

The car traffic below was made to pause:
And some nice people helped to form a cordon
Beneath the man, and others gave applause
To him, though he was now the city's burden.

And all along the tightrope, winds of change
Caused ripples in the rope, but Johnny's leap
Was some two hundred yards, caught by this strange
Springboard, which bounced him back toward the rope

Five times, until he landed on his head,
Caught headlong in the turmoil of the crowds.
They lifted him away, then home to bed—
Where finally he slept, and dreamed of clouds...

The gargoyle

The gargoyle gurgles, set in stone;
A frozen gremlin, someone's clone,
But frazzled with those pointy ears—
A creature that's been there for years.

I drink my coffee walking past,
And wonder whether time at last
Will free him from his solid state,
And all his lies regurgitate.

Beach ball play

Lonely, I wandered through the beach,
Throwing along my big beach ball:
It flew, it drifted out of reach,
And over those strewn, I stood tall;

They cluttered sands, lying so sweet
And staring out into the waves,
Under umbrellas, in this heat;
People who lay, as in their graves,

All ready to be buried there;
And as the wind let fly my ball,
It bounced among them—most did stare,
But some people cared not at all.

The ball, it landed in the lap
Of a most gorgeous lady lying;
I looked into her luscious gap,
And she could see how I was prying—

To my surprise she hooked the ball
Between her knees, and swayed a dance:
Much like a seal, she let it fall
Then brought it back in solid stance;

And I did backflips up the beach,
And down to where the lady lay,
Big smiles between us each to each,
In this rambunctious beach ball play.

Widdershins

This word, it means "to travel round
Counter to workings of a clock".
Many of us elders do abound
Who, whether in search of place or sock

Or just a spot to rest our bums—
Whatever it is, my story's this:
One day, poking my head for plums
Atop a tree, I reached in bliss,

But one plum fell straight to the ground,
Hitting a land-mine in the zone—
And other than that massive sound,
I knew part of my leg had blown—

Of course, I yelled and cursed the war,
And clung to dear life anyhow:
My left leg, bandaged, very sore,
Was hardly good for walking now—

Long story short, I now leaned left,
And learned to walk in counter-spins;
And though it seems a bit bereft,
I now swear by my widdershins.

I did not see the cat

I did not see the cat play dead.
I did not see her on my head—

I did not see her hide inside
My newest hairdo wild and wide.

I did not hear her caterwaul,
Nor see the scratches in the hall;

I did not see her kill the mouse,
And hide the body 'neath the house.

I did not give her balls of yarns
Stored up in Grandma's giant barns,

Nor see her with her claws destroy
Gran's crochet, with a look so coy,

So evil on this Black Friday:
Though evidence of it there lay...

Nor leap off Grandma's rocking-chair,
I did not see her anywhere—

I did not see her tip the vase
Of flowers, or upset the jars,

Or scowl to spy the neighbor's cat,
Or hide under the tall top hat—

All that I saw was clearly that:
The cat sat on the mat.

Between the shelves

As I strolled cautiously about
The shelves of books, my keen eyes lingered
On some strange titles, which I doubt
I'd seen before, or once had fingered;

My eyes lost focus, and my thought
Did gravitate to years ago,
When I was just a youngster caught
In books that many didn't know;

Like butterflies or dust, my eyes
Did set upon a face behind
The books: I did slowly surmise
It was a friend I'd had in mind.

Her eyes met mine, and she withdrew
Her face between these books so wild;
Before she disappeared from view,
I saw her smile, as once she'd smiled;

And if it were polite t' exclaim
In such a place, I would have made
A fond hello, recalled her name,
Instead of this unkind charade.

Her worms and her squirms

My squeamy sister eating worms and worms
Laced with those sugars—sour, wormy types—
Stuck in her queensize bed, she squirms and squirms,
Her body fraught, her hands with blanket gripes—

And then, in wayward scenes, she screams and screams,
Gnashing and clawing, biting with her teeth—
A nine-year harbinger of horrid dreams,
Clutching her brightly colored worms beneath—

Her stare, her cold adrenaline, her mouth
Stained red, her bitterness of life itself,
Speaks quietly to me of things uncouth,
And all the things she raided off the shelf;

And then—she stops, and drops her fuming head,
Hiding under the pillow all her pains,
Only to watch old *Star Wars* scenes instead—
Using the "Force", while nighttime darkness reigns.

Pig over the oceans

Upon a makeshift raft, I paddled out
From island shores, with nothing but my pig,
The clothes I wore, and one bottle of stout—
And on an empty stomach took a swig,

And soon after, realised that wasn't smart;
For suddenly, the winds and rains arose:
The storm swelled, my poor raft soon broke apart;
Yet would I save the pig, and his pink nose?

Yes! as the ocean rocked and rolled my soul,
All through this storm, this ocean's cold abyss,
I breathed into my pig, who remained whole—
Protecting him...but did I mention this?:

My pig was not a real pig, but a toy:
Inflatable, yet Chinese-made to last;
And he became my savior, my life's buoy;
So through this storm I, still drunk, held him fast;

And as I clung, the stars shone brighter yet
And winked at me, now floating with my boar,
Whom I held dear, and held in my life's debt,
Until I washed up safely back to shore.

Oh yes! I ended up in China, where
The folks were friendly—now, safe from my strife,
I drank in celebration, and with care,
In honor of the pig who saved my life.

Me, the old man, and the kite

The old man held me tight, so tight,
Then let me just a little loose—
Not, as I thought, a ghost's vamoose—
So I could just a little linger,
And wound the string around my finger,
That let me dance my air-flung kite;

Then held me tight again, his eyes
Receptive to the wind, the skies,
Then let me loose, stood back again,
Despite the folds of sleet or rain,
While my kite jigged and danced and leapt;
And cold and wet, the old man kept

As still as any stone, for death
Awaiting like the Earth's dull breath,
Groaning amid the youthful dance
Of my bright kite, and its slight chance,
And I, intent to keep the flight,
Stood not too heavy, or too light.

The adept percussionist

He plays the timpani so well:
A roll, a rumble, and a swell—
The augur of the deathly boom,
Its final note, ultimate doom.

He then picks up the triangle,
A little tinkle here and there,
Grinning like a stranded angel,
Fragile as priceless glassware.

When that is done, the man assumes
The pair of golden cymbals now:
A clashing gust below the nose,
Dashing the ears with strong elbows!
Or, pearled with sound, how it illumes
Its shimmeringly golden glow.

The mad man at christmas

It is, it is a christmas of clichés:
The glitter, carols, bright lights, flashing toys—
And from the roaming crowds, a soft malaise;
O wild Australia, its silver joys.

And inside one of those expansive malls,
The mad man rages, letting it all go,
And all the more, between these concrete walls—
Screaming and screaming, about his AVO*—

Ambling to and fro, as onlookers but stare,
They're dumbstruck as a bell-less Tinkerbell
Caught in the headlights of his sudden glare—
As he pursues that winding path to hell.

*Apprehended Violence Order

The televised lovers

He watches them oozing in love,
Drifting as on a heav'nly boat—
Records them, sitting perched above—
So silent, but for his long gloat.

He sees him stroke her legs so lean,
Which bend, rising to meet his arm,
And as they cuddle close between
The windows, he sounds the alarm!

So as the loudspeaker blares out,
"Evacuate!", the two look blank,
Still naked, still quite lost in doubt,
And naive to this devious prank—

And yet, this rank, strange intercourse
Is being broadcast to Channel Four—
The comedy special's *tour de force*,
Livestreamed from door to door.

Who stole my hat?

In swift parade, pushed by the crowd,
I dropped the hat that made me proud:
Plush head of one great unicorn,
With rainbow swirls upon her horn—

I'd made it by myself, so keen,
Using my home sewing machine,
And wore it almost everyday,
Prancing around all o'er the fray,

And when I lost it, through my haste
I could not find it 'mongst the waste
Of that ol' grand parade, that day:
I stood there, lost in my dismay,

E'en when the crowds had long gone home;
So when I went to school next time,
My friends noticed my hat was gone,
Replaced by my big frown, forlorn.

One day, however, in the town,
Months later, some stray kid unknown
Was wearing my exact same hat!
I went up to him, said, "Hey what!

"That hat looks just like mine I lost!"
He said: "I bought it at a cost."
He would not give it back, O nay!
I grabbed him, but he ran away!

And so the world looked very grim,
To know the hat belonged to HIM,
But yesterday I saw another:
My SAME HAT worn by some GRANDMOTHER!!

Whether the same as that before,
I could not be especially sure,
And so...I went home, and to bed,
Putting my pillow on my head.

The street broker

With saucy mouth and crooked nose,
He stoops to eavesdrop, I suppose,
As businessmen now trickle out
Onto the busy walkabout—

He's dirty, but the men are clean;
He's got the grease, and in between
Their ideas, he now makes his move:
Some coins for a joke, or a jig or a groove?

He's very eager then to please,
Prepared to ask on what's "For Lease",
Something to do, or place to stay,
In this real-life Monopoly?

He saws the air explaining things,
And all the "profit" that it brings;
Mansplaining, with his airy bends,
Insurance, trusts, and market trends.

But those men, grim-faced, play no fools:
And so, as this hot pavement cools,
The coy man starts to edge away
Into the vastness of the day.

The zebra in the city

Zebra! zebra! trotting, trotting past:
Lights, the signs, and many buildings vast;
People staring, taking photo snaps
Of you walking along between the gaps,

Poking your flaring, puffing nostrils at
Streaming fast cars, all their empty cheers
Ringing in your dainty ears, but that
Your pretty onyx eyes are glazed with tears—

With a most fearful flutter, you step out
Onto the zebra crossing, as a Porsche
Swiftly approaches—with a sudden shout
The driver fails to see you, O my gosh!

You're black and white alone upon this path,
Crushed by this racecar, kicking, as your blood
Flows from your side in this cold aftermath:
Spurting, and gushing onto that car's hood—

The driver splutters, coming out at last,
Still fumbling for his phone, to call someone;
While swelling crowds of humans stand aghast
At your precious soul's death, already done.

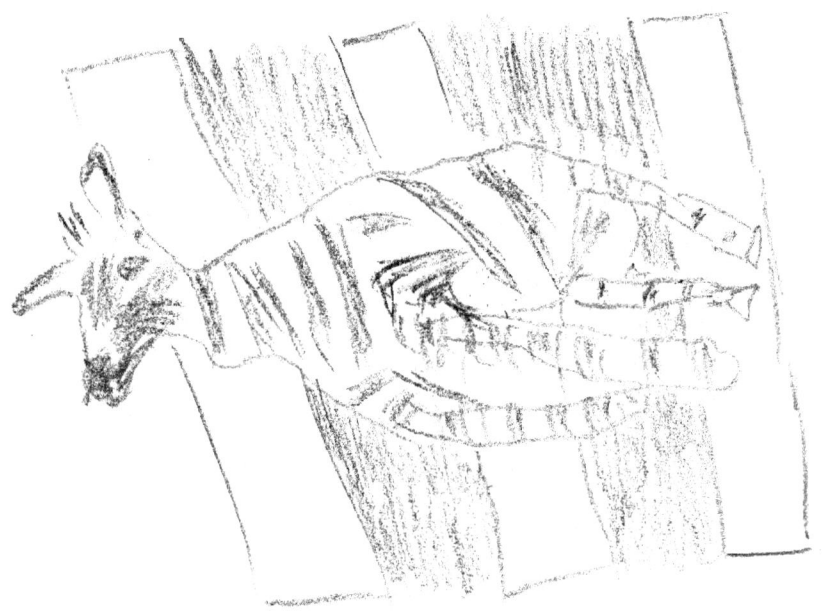

A realist's valentine poem

Roses are red, and violets are violet,
They're growing above my ol' gurgling toilet;
I always step next door to access the shower,
And sing a sweet song for my every flower.

And likewise, if I see you out of the blue
Coming rushing to see me, or to use my loo,
I'll blow you a kiss, like the wandering dew,
And let you inside, for a moment or two.

Rapacious pizza

With planted fingers, and with eyes,
A piece of pizza I do prise,
With stalagmites and stalagbites
My face smiles, filled with vagaries;

It's full of flavour, full of fire,
So full of pulling-out desire;
The saucy turnings of my tongue,
The devilled triangles require;

But others come to hoard this treasure,
Shared among all by some poor measure:
The empty box somewhere is flung,
And stomach gropes remain our pleasure.

The poisoned fish

At her vast table—perched upon her chair,
Though eating had become so hard for her—
Of th' creature's bulging eyes and silken skin,
Morsel by forked morsel, she stuffed it in.

In her vain thoughts, the poor fish seemed to swim:
Though she was conscious, th' room lights seemed to dim,
Though the consumer, she felt all-consumed,
Sickened, fatigued, and poisoned—somehow, doomed.

And oh! she gasped for water, or clean air,
Or anything that would relieve her pain—
But nothing would work—she, clutching her hair,
Or rushing to the loo, and back again—

And in her dreams, the fish snapped at her face,
Saying, "Be sorry, though I have no voice;
We both did suffer, though you held the ace:
Buggered by fish fork, and your own life's choice."

The man from Timbuktu

He's all the way from Timbuktu,
Reading the scriptures torn apart,
So old, with friends scattered and few,
And foodstuffs careful to compart.

And now, somehow, he's standing by,
Arrived safely at our North Pole.
Maybe he dropped out of the sky,
Escaped from customs rigmarole.

Or maybe he swam many miles
Through waves and all the rain's downpour,
Ignored by many sharks, whose smiles
Guided him on to reach this shore.

I feel that luck is on his side,
But he must learn to live anew:
Trying in this snowstorm to hide,
His feet stick out of his igloo.

Rules of the snack machine

Somewhere, nestled on these stolen lands,
In some state, the finest museum stands:
And—there stands (to one side, on level four)
A snack machine, next to the dinosaur.

(For each item, you have to pay the price.
That's what the dino says. He's not that nice.)
So when you have the munchies, you go there,
To get some crisps, or soda—but beware!

The legend says that if you rock the joint,
Wobble the snack machine, or stick a point
Inside, you'll lose whatever you have paid,
And some alarm will sound, I am afraid,

And you'll look bad—and dino will get mad,
As many earthquakes form below your feet,
Causing extinction, or the curse of gad—
So please, obey the sign, and never cheat.

Appraising the statues

She looks the real layered babushka,
Alighting from the busy train;
Who follows in its wake and woosh-ka,
And looks behind herself again;

Who hobbles down the flight of stairs,
Earnest and firm in her regard,
Gripping your strong arm unawares,
To pull you away and far backward;

And if she cannot source the pity
Of some stranger, she'll go alone
To th' vast bronze statues of the city,
That stand aloof, above this crone

Whose arms brush off the pigeons, flung
From her knees, toes and nobbled nose,
Unlike the statues, taking dung
From every bird perched on their pose;

And she, like water wrung from stone,
Weeps long into the city's grey,
Her vision blurred, her love ingrown
Upon these statues, in dismay.

The lost mathematical proof

The young maths whiz, who with a squizz
Found flaws in every argument,
Just to remove from common tizz,
She did headstands to circumvent:

Down at the local shops, she stood
Upon her head for many hours,
Wherein she solved, by rule or rood,
Fermat's Last Theorem, with its powers.

She righted herself for a moment,
And scribbled the solution down
On papers, in ev'ry component:
Made certain, proven, deftly shown.

But just as she was good to choof,
Some street kids held her at knifepoint,
And took her satchel, with the proof
She'd done in such precise adjoint.

The thieves had no idea they'd seized
A million-dollar document;
They took her cash, and were too pleased
To chuck the satchel down a vent:

Down, down the drain to that town's sewer,
Where it lay washed beneath those slats;
It rotted, festered, lost for ever—
Until it was devoured by rats.

The terrarium experiment

It was a simple joke at first—
The plants required, for their thirst,
Some rainwater to just feel fresh—
But Sammy fed them lumps of flesh

From his "Muckdonalds" Happy Meal,
Which, over weeks, did quite congeal
And emanate their ugly odor,
And each plant did a huge exploder!

They grew shoots out of their glass bowl,
And ate all things, like some black hole,
Till Tammy had to trim them back,
Using some sharp scissors to hack;

And mould now grew inside the glass,
Becoming lumps of some large mass,
Until Sam brought some slugs to roost,
But then Tam gave them "Superboost",

Some very costly fertiliser;
And Sammy, who was none the wiser,
Gave them some seaweed and some kelp,
Hoping that it would somehow help.

It did—the plants started to bloom
Into a thousand little buds,
Until there was not even room
(Like Noah's Ark in the Great Floods)—

And since the bowl hung by a chain,
One day the chain broke and, like rain,
The bowl crashed to the studio floor,
Smashing to bits, staining decor!

Poor Sam and Tam (I must confess),
They wanted of this nothing more.
But too scared to clean up their mess,
They slipped away, closing the door.

So next time you feed stuff to plants,
Or keep their bowl but grow their size,
Remember they could be mutants—
You could be in for some surprise!

The forlorn seamstress

She sits before the sewing machine,
For the 15-thousandth time:
This is the place she's always been
With every reason, every rhyme.

And as the shudders of the work
Echo upon this factory floor,
She dreams of freedom, with a smirk,
And of the most noble folklore:

Of rags to riches, and of bitches
Who marry into pristine wealth:
Nothing of sewing or of stitches—
Good life, good tiding, and good health.

And as her fingers start their itches,
She gets back to her simple work:
The finishing of these fine britches,
To be worn by some county clerk.

Rising of the phoenix

A most majestic bird,
That slept for forty days on their own turd.

Oh did they struggle,
Struggle, struggle to be even heard.

Oh were they burnt:
Once, twice, and more, a lesson learnt.

In flames, they wept
The tears that motioned how they leapt.

The flames looked funny;
And the tears that put them out were runny.

They died, the end:
They lost both self, and love, and friend.

And in that end, rebirth:
They found their true and noble worth.

Man changes lightbulb

He hunts about the garage walls
For one replacement bulb, a 60-watt:
And as the leaden twilight falls,
He still can't find one, 60-watt or not;

And now he scrabbles in the dark,
The clutter, stench, debris, and, looking out,
Imagines *Hunting of the Snark*—
With all his many items knocked about—

Trips on a wire, hits his head
Upon the nearest shelf, from which there falls
A box of christmas lights instead:
And merrily adorns his house's halls

With these amazing colors, hot
And wild; and with a knowing little smirk,
Rubs ointment on his head's sore spot,
And goes to sleep before he goes to work.

Most ridiculous recipe

A sub gum stew, of many things,
I'll now concoct, what joy it brings!
These long rats' tails, those crickets' wings,
The caviar of underlings!

The sloughed skin of a shiny snake,
Into the pot we'll boil and bake,
The abscess of a screaming pig,
And blood sluiced from a whaler rig,

Tongue of green frog stung by a prong,
Foie gras made like there's nothing wrong,
The eye of squid, bloodshot and raw,
The poo of which we shall ignore!

Oh, master chef, how did you find
Each rare ingredient assigned?
—Haha, says he, I didn't—yet
I own a greenhouse hot and wet

That grows ten thousand different plants—
So, seriously, what's the chance
You're eating something JUST AS NICE
for less than half the starting price?!

I've used herbs, spices, flowers, buds,
Fresh vegetables, like beets and spuds,
And many different parts thereof...
It's all VEGAN, and made with LOVE.

The diners dropped their silent jaws,
And some tried vomiting, because
They *thought* the man had cooked them shit,
And THEY just could not handle it...!

The wandering piper

O do you hear the piper playing, wand'ring round our town?
He pokes his head round every corner, piping up and down;
And all along the rustic streets, d'you hear his floating tune?
Echoed in toilet cubicles, he plays the *Clair de Lune*!

He wanders in the hair salon, inspiring all the girls,
His melody enchanting, wafting, in such pretty curls;
Then struts along the tired pavements, rousing beggars lying,
Whereon he stops to talk with them, a musicked angel sighing.

At lunchtimes, between scattered kids, inspiring them to jig,
He strides between these scallywags, riding their whirligig;
He walks afar and plays to imitate the city's glow,
Filling up fields and houses with proud notes in every row.

One day, he tries to pass the concrete buildings near the morgue,
And find himself inside a heavy meeting (pimps dot org):
And as he starts his tune, the fat suits rattle him with bellows:
He backs off with, "Forgive my trespass," ending all his hellos;

And pushed backward, he swoons as their thick door slams in his face!
Turning around, he hides his pipe and lopes off in disgrace!
Outside, a traffic jam, with drivers yelling through the smoke,
Blasting their horns and stereo beats, with reason to provoke!

The piper sits upon the curb and, lo, begins to weep;
Then paces swiftly o'er the crystal mountains very steep,
And silently closes his books of musical memoirs,
And hides his teary face among a multitude of stars.

The old man's will

He ran his bottom lip across the envelope,
Sealing the document, and his conceit, within;
His eye then rose, like some old telescope,
And then he spoke (his voice was very thin):

"I think that with my life's secrets, it's better
They should be buried with my cold dead soul—
Except with this: the last, one, final letter,
Which will this puzzle make, again, one whole."

He then planted the letter in the safe,
And closed the lock, which shuddered with a "clack";
And by the fire, his hands rubbed to chafe
His thudding heart, then thumped me on the back:

"The final verse of my life's song is sung,
Whatever my last month, or year, becomes—
Yet you, my younger son, whilst not so young,
For all your lifelong troubles, shall get crumbs—"

My eyes lit up, and I was sore aggrieved;
I grabbed my old man by the neck, and cried:
"You stingy man! That I am so bereaved—
Give me my fair share—give me back my pride!"

The old man choked, and tried to free my grasp,
And fell into a fit, coughing to drown
From smoking for such years—his voice's rasp
Could only blurt out, "Please, son, put me down!!...

"My fortune's mostly for your own incomes,
But so's the junk, the porn, the bits 'n' pieces,
All trinkets from the past, and all the crumbs!
They will be yours, when your old man deceases!"

And so, with this slow realisation spreading
Across my face, the old man gently sighed:
By some sixth sense, he knew where this was heading...
And in my arms, he gasped, and softly died.

About the creator

MARCUS TEN LOW (born 1979) is an ecologist, poet, and artivist who aspires to be "kind to all beings", currently living on unceded Jagera and Turrbal land. The creator of the *Veegan Planet* comic series and the inventor of the dubious concept known as #livingmodelling, he has also been published many times by *Quadrant, The Big Issue* (Australia), and the Animal Justice Party (Qld, Australia). He failed at tertiary level on several occasions and has been incarcerated in Australia on more than 20 occasions. @antibreeder1m, his social media actively promotes causes to mitigate the world's imminent destruction.

www.ingramcontent.com/pod-product-compliance
Lightning Source LLC
Chambersburg PA
CBHW040318170426
43197CB00021B/2957